LIBRA
HOROSCOPE
2020

Libra Horoscope

2020

Copyright © 2019 Mystic Cat

All rights reserved. This book or any portion thereof may not be reproduced or used in any manner whatsoever without the express written permission of the publisher except for the use of brief quotations in a book review.

The information accessible from this book is for informational purposes only. None of the data within should be regarded as a promise of benefits, a claim of cures, a statutory warranty, or a guarantee of results to be achieved.

The images are used under license from Shutterstock, Dreamstime, or Deposit-photos.

Libra

Libra Dates: September 23 to October 22
Symbol: Scales
Element: Air
Planet: Venus
House: Seventh
Colors: Ivory, pink, light-blue

JANUARY HOROSCOPE

ASTROLOGICAL & ZODIAC ENERGY

OBSERVANT ~ TECHNICAL ~ PATIENT

WORK & CAREER

There is some restructuring going on, which has your situation focusing on the bottom line. The company is looking for people who are dedicated, loyal, and committed to the company. Concentrate on applying your talents at the highest level will help you shine and draw security into your working life. You may even score a new role, which elevates your situation. It leads to a productive and active phase in the chapter ahead. Your ability to think on your feet, and turn a challenge into an advantage, hold you in good stead. It does show you are ready to make strides at improving your working environment. Your job is richly rewarding, this inspires you to heighten the productivity, and grow your role. You can rise above uncertainty, and this provides you with the chance to build strong foundations, a methodical and meticulous approach draws abundance. You turn the tides in your favor; your ability to tackle challenging progress resonates with your ability to handle the demands which cross your path. It combines beautifully with your desire to improve your working situation. Your qualities are noticed by those who can influence your future working life. It does enable you to establish yourself in a more stable environment. A harbor of bustling activity leads to forward progress. Setting intentions for the path forward does bring qualities of manifestation into your world. The Friday the 10th Full moon in Cancer coincides with a lunar eclipse. This brings an emotional element into your life; it has you tapping into a deeper awareness around your working goals. It's an essential month for plotting the course ahead; you plant the seedlings of aspirations, which blossom over the coming months. The lunar New Year occurs on the 25th of January, this is the Chinese year of the Rat, an auspicious year which offers you plenty of luck and good fortune in 2020.

LOVE & ROMANCE

Couples

Information is the currency that brings this situation to a new level. A conversation ahead enables a secret to be revealed. It brings luck into your life, you build a foundation which offers you room to draw abundance into your world. It does have you thinking about the potential possible. There is an undercurrent of potential which surrounds you, a hum of creative energy sends ripples of curiosity into your life. That has you exploring new options, you embrace a chapter which sees the excitement and inspiration figure prominently in your world. It does support a steady cycle of growth and leads to a more social environment. This shapes a new world of potential for your social life.

Singles

You hear news about a social event that captures your interest. It does have you configuring your life to open your world to these types of opportunities. It provides you with an option to embrace a more social chapter. Stepping into your own confidence, you make smart decisions that provide you with new potential. It is a fruitful time, you pave the way forward, and embrace a busy and productive time. You may be feeling restless, ready to create the space necessary to expand your life. Changes ahead stoke your vision; it puts the spotlight on improving your social experience; this increases emotional harmony and illuminates a chapter of new options that shift your focus forwards. It is a hectic and active time ahead, channeling your energy into a situation which inspires your mind, does reveal a closer bond is possible with someone who catches your eye.

IDEAS & CREATIVITY

There are changes ahead which have you feeling more settled, it does see you making strides towards improving your circumstances. As you overcome limitations, you release areas that have held back progress. This holds you in good stead, you discover a path which offers golden nuggets, it inspires your mind to take a risk and dive into a new area. It does see things shaping up nicely in the chapter ahead. There's a lot of potential emerging in your life over the coming months, long-term goals begin to take shape, you gain clarity into the path ahead. It does see your ability to create positive change is heightened. This sees you entering new territory;

it gives you a chance to expand your horizons and discover a path that offers you room to grow your life. It is an environment that draws a nice boost into your world. Changes are coming, it sets off a pathway which enables you to make progress. You forge a path, which is food for your soul. It does show a patient and flexible approach, indeed draws dividends.

Issues & Hurdles

There is an emphasis on nurturing your life as you are ending a phase, there may be some healing and processing of emotions during this time. If you do feel more sensitive than usual, don't fight these feelings, create space to resolve, and release energy, which no longer serves your higher purpose. You have learned harsh lessons, you now know, to set the bar higher, and to be discerning. Your ability to nut out and choose the right situation is instrumental in obtaining your vision. You have an uncanny ability to cut through to the heart of the matter. It helps you spot the disingenuous people, and enables you to focus your energy on developing transparent bonds. There is some mixing of high power, this is true, co-workers and associates may feel competitive, this is because it is evident that your star shines brightly. Perseverance and dedication will establish a firm base. An offer crosses your path, it does shine a curious spotlight on improving a situation that had been problematic. You enter a phase that lets you accomplish a great deal of growth. It is a compelling chapter, the actions you take draw new options into your world. Making yourself a priority is precisely the recipe for success. It is an intense phase of following your heart and moving in alignment with your intuition. This expands your vision of what is possible for you this Chinese year of the Rat, which begins on the 25th of January.

FEBRUARY HOROSCOPE

ASTROLOGICAL THEME & ZODIAC ENERGY

MAGNETIC ~ ADVENTUROUS ~ INVOLVED

WORK & CAREER

The beginning of February is a time of steady progress for Libra. Some gains are made, this gives you a strong indication of what can be achieved throughout this year. The first Supermoon for 2020 occurs in your sign on February 9th. You enter a time that offers room to progress your career goals. It does see you obtaining a vision which draws security, it focuses on developing emotional foundations, as you set down your goals, you connect with one who brings stability into your life. You have grown resilient and adaptable through the changes which have occurred over the years. It holds you in good stead to make the most of the option ahead. It is a journey of a lifetime, it's going to take you places, and nurturing these gifts will see them grow. You have the core abilities, developing the skills further will see your star rise. It is a month of progress, change, and movement. You discover much is possible in this active environment. It does help you progress a career goal, you embrace a more self-expression time, and feel that you are given the green light to gain traction on your vision. You discover that the times are changing, you don't take things too seriously, your ability to be adaptable, and go with the flow enables you to make strides on improving your situation. It does see life is dynamic. A new case comes to light, which offers you room to grow a personal goal. This is an area that inspires your mind and has you thinking about the potential possible. It does see enthusiasm blossom in your world. Making the right moves sets the tone ahead. It offers you a chance to grow your career path. Additionally, the new moon in Aquarius on the 23rd brings clarity. This information brings with it rejuvenating energy to help stabilize you over the Mercury retrograde phase.

LOVE & ROMANCE

Couples

It is a time that draws a blend of manifestation into your personal life. A close bond is deepened, an exciting opportunity to plot a course towards long-term goals for mutual gain leads to an exciting chapter of planning and strategy. Unexpected news arrives to light a path forward, it is harboring change and growth. Everything takes on a glow of inspiration, bringing a river of potential into your life. This person is an optimistic individual who harnesses a positive approach to life's problems. Whatever challenges they come across, they see it as a challenge, and their innovative and energetic mind soon arrives at a suitable solution. They have a passion for life, an inherent excitement about future possibilities. This is someone who enjoys trying new things, and discovering what lay on the off the beaten path. This person is a natural adventurer, they have a visionary nature who enjoys movement and new experiences. You are his life and soul, his hearty companion, while he doesn't like to be pinned down, this one appreciates having the security of a relationship.

Singles

A celebration is in the air when attractive news crosses your path. It does see a social environment; a gateway to new potential brings opportunities to make life brighter. There is a social gathering which crops up; attending this event puts you in contact with like-minded individuals. It's a wonderful time that coaxes you out of your usual routine and allows you to dive into a community event. You are set to benefit from news, which provides you with insight into your situation. It does enable you to capitalize on fresh energy; it puts you in the box seat to land in an environment which is ripe for romantic potential. Focusing on self-development opens your world to new opportunities. You are ready to shift your situation forward. Setting aspirations to expand your horizons does create a potent phase of potential. It leads to a refreshing time, it draws lively interactions, and does provide a landscape which is ripe for mining new friendships. You move forward more consciously and confidently towards developing your personal goals.

Ideas & Creativity

During the February 9th Supermoon in Leo, you unwrap a cycle of new creative energy. It is time for you to shine. You are bold, audacious, daring, and capable. It gives you a fantastic opportunity to utilize your creative side and fan the flames of potential. It does leave you feeling inspired, you are on a mission to make a statement which impacts your working environment, you certainly succeed. You make strides on improving your situation, shaking off the doubt, connecting with the broader world of opportunity, you soon discover a path that offers room to grow your vision. It does draw happiness and abundance. Being open to change is a crucial element that enables you to pursue your goals. A decision made soon kick-starts a dynamic phase of growth. It sees you pressing forwards towards obtaining a lofty vision. You can create significant change, staying on top of your game, you draw active energy into your life. It lets you break free of constraints, the winds of change sweep into your life. It opens a gateway that brings abundance into your world. You receive the news soon, which sweeps in with exciting potential. It has you thinking about future possibilities, you soon scope out a plan, and begin to make strides towards making your vision happen. It is a time of increasing self-expression and creativity. You are headed towards an extensive chapter which offers rejuvenation, on the grand scheme of things, it enables you to fully engage with life and increase the abundance flowing into your world. You discover that stress levels are lower, no longer triggered by events that used to disrupt your energy, you take time to appreciate the blessings, it enables you to open your heart to a happy chapter. A surprise arrives to give you a boost soon.

There is an impressive total of 4 supermoons in 2020. The more you tune into it, the more you are aware that you are going in the right direction. Your ideas blossom under the power of these supermoons.

Issues & Hurdles

Focusing on the past muddies the water of clarity, it prevents you from moving forward in your life. This is a time where you may feel motivated to really look at the direction ahead, as you face the crossroads, a decision made during this time will be instrumental in improving things. There are many changes ahead that revolutionize your life. It does see some essential re-configurations occurring in your life. This could easily send you in a different direction. It does see conversations ahead, which set the stage for future progress. A situation you pour your energy into soon ignites with passion. Your current location will be tested, your future goals could be at odds with your current location. Letting go of limitations, letting go of fear, guilt, and doubt, you don't have a fixed destination in mind; you take a broader perspective. One thing is for sure, the area you feed will grow. Look at the direction you wish to nurture, plant the seed you seek to blossom. You have more control over the path ahead than you may currently realize. The winds of change sweep in to shift you forward. You are more confident about what you need in your life. Asserting your authority enables you to set appropriate boundaries. It does catapult you away from a lingering situation, it sees you blazing through a time of reconnecting with a broader world of opportunity. This kicks off a cycle that inspires you to follow your heart and live your passion.

MARCH HOROSCOPE

ASTROLOGICAL THEME & ZODIAC ENERGY

PROGRESSIVE ~ FREE-SPIRITED ~ EXPERIENTIAL

WORK & CAREER

The Full Moon in Virgo is another supermoon this month. As the season changes, so do your situation. Change can happen in many ways, change can fix your current location, or change can completely revolutionize your life and create radical change. Stretch past your comfort zone and introduce yourself to new friends or like-minded people, and the area you feed takes flight. It opens up a fresh cycle of opportunity. It does make things to a more secure and stable environment. And this brings things together nicely, you discover harmony, and the ability to structure long-term plans.

All in all, it does suggest a positive result is possible. It's a situation that has so much potential; it needs the timing to be right. You are doing the right thing by exploring options. Changes ahead help put you on the right path to grow your career. You don't want to be stuck in a dead-end role where they undervalue your abilities. Your dedication, perseverance, and resilience hold you in good stead, an offer crosses your path, doing due diligence, enables you to see clearly the right way to take. It unleashes you in an environment that is ripe to progress your goals. Events on the horizon do help you gain insight into a situation of interest. It feeds your intellectual mind with inspiring new options. It does see you gaining traction on a career goal, this has you feeling ready to put your vision into practice. It does suggest your efforts to improve your situation offer you incredible advancement. You soon begin to wonder why you doubted in the first place, and the area you nourish takes flight.

LOVE & ROMANCE

Couples

It does have you thinking about the past and the memories you treasure. It creates space to nurture your world, and there is plenty to celebrate, as when you nurture your energy, you create the right environment to draw new options into your world. Change soon sweeps in. A situation, you nurture ignites with new potential. It does enable things to flow forward naturally. This person takes the time to build foundations that are practical and grounded. It is a time that is fun-loving, adventurous, and endearing. It brings beautiful sparks into your world and places a strong emphasis on improving your personal life. You do see the situation evolving, moving towards a closer bond. It does bring change and excitement, you begin a voyage which highlights exploring the possibilities with this person. It drives a time of wanderlust, their opportunities ahead to deepen the bond with this person, you do get feedback from them, it helps you know that you are on the right path towards developing a closer connection.

Singles

Events in your local community could turn up some new friends soon. Spending time with kindred spirits draws lively discussions, attractive opportunities to bond, which brings abundance into your world. A gathering at your local catch up area does bring fantastic potential, it introduces you to someone you relate well with. It does see a situation moving beyond small talk and gathering pace. Your personal life heats up with enticing new potential. A shift forward is coming to your social life. It does see a budding romance picking up speed. You enter an auspicious chapter which sees an enticing situation deepening, you embrace this lively time, it launches you towards developing a bond which captures your inspiration. Staying open to new potential, lights a path forward towards romance and adventure. It is a time that reveals hidden information. Seeing the truth of the situation does help you discover a new possibility. A secret admirer steps up soon and has a conversation that gets the ball rolling towards developing a deeper bond. This does give you food for thought, it could lead to a close alliance being forged, lively time of romance and adventure beckons.

IDEAS & CREATIVITY

You are ready to explore exciting far-flung destinations; you discover a breakthrough that enables you to grow your situation. The goals you investigate turn out to be well worth your energy. It does see things going smoothly as you unwrap a cycle which offers you progression. It is a time of revealing new treasures, you have plenty to be excited about over the coming months. You can create space to nurture your goals, you discover a situation that ramps up with exciting potential. As you find the breakthrough you had hoped to see, you begin to uncover an area that draws happiness, it has taken some time to come together, but it's all about to happen for you. It leads to a time of future planning and goal setting. This is a time that gives rise to new ambitions; you feel the fever pitch of a new phase that offers you a chance to develop a situation that captures your mind and inspiration. It does catapult you towards a fantastic aspect of growth. Good news is coming, this governs an expansive chapter, it does create an outlet where you can focus your excess energy into. Your perseverance, persistence, and discipline are rewarded when a project which is undertaken takes on new potential. It is a time of transformation, as a sweet offer crosses your path, this provides you with an option, you can develop further. It leads to an exciting time when you get a broader sense of what can be achieved.

ISSUES & HURDLE

Healing is a substantial aspect of the first part of March. Mercury retrograde ends on Monday 9th, and communication issues should improve soon after. It does also see the second super moon arriving on the same day. This full Moon in Virgo helps you tap into your emotional awareness. It brings you to a time of clearing away the blockages and letting go of outworn energy. It is a time which can feel sentimental, nostalgia makes an entrance turning your vision back to past events. This slows you down so that you can process the shifting sands of time, and integrate the memories into your heart which you treasure so dearly. The past has been a treasure trove of learning, it helped shape the person you are today, you can value the lessons learned, and utilize them effectively to improve your current situation. In fact, it is a great time to expand your horizons and dive into a new area. Some seeds which are planted over the next month blossom into something significant; it enables you to harness the power within and bring creative ideas to life. The past is a time which holds many treasured memories, it has been an extraordinary time of learning and growth. You're currently in the midst of an intensely insightful transformation, it has you delving deep, and obtain substantial benefits by focusing on developing your inherent gifts. As you continue to build your world, you are going to connect with others on a similar path, it does see you mingling with eclectic spirits who engage fully with life. One thing is for sure, expanding your horizons draws a happier chapter. It marks a transition that closes the door on a problematic area. It instigates an active phase of healing, and this enables you to shift your focus towards a vision of abundance. You've known the trials and hurdles, now you can open a gateway towards joy.

APRIL HOROSCOPE

ASTROLOGICAL THEME & ZODIAC ENERGY

LIVELY ~ OPEN ~ GUTSY

WORK & CAREER

You have been in a time of transformation, the Full Moon in Libra on 8th of April is a supermoon, it's also known as Hunters Moon, as your life moves forward, there is a strong emphasis on achieving growth. It takes you to a significant turning point, standing at the crossroads, you may feel unsure of the direction ahead. Setting a course for a path that is by your higher goals does keep life moving smoothly forward. You can set a course for a busy time ahead. It does take you on a transformational trajectory, it harnesses a sense of vitality, you can utilize dynamic energy to achieve an active phase of growth. It does invite expansion into your life, your curious mind seeks to dive deeply into new territory. It does see plenty of options emerging which feed your account with fresh inspiration. Your fortune is on the rise, you shift towards expansion and engage with the broader world of potential. It does take you to an exciting time of exploring new options, the crux of this chapter is about shifting your focus towards change, you have set a goal in your mind, and you radiate a frequency which enables this to manifest in due course. You discover a situation that is on offer, taking a leap of faith that you dive into fresh territory.

LOVE & ROMANCE

Couples

This connection can reveal potential when the time is right to progress it further. By being flexible, you let the situation unfurl gently; this creates stable foundations from which to advance your vision. It does see the future shimmers with new possibilities; it offers you a chance to develop a closer bond with this person, leading to an exciting chapter of new options. Your patience and flexibility reward you with an open book of exciting potential. It does see a shift forward, this brings things together nicely, you plumb new depths of emotional bonding with this person. It does recognize there is an undercurrent of possibility ready to blossom, it sets the stage for an impressive outcome to unfold further down the track. It awakens you to the increasing abundance, which is seeking to tempt you forward.

Singles

If things have felt restless on the romance front, the single and looking Cancerian can expect a new flow of energy to sweep when the supermoon in Libra occurs on the 8th of April. This incredible full moon helps shift things forward. There will be opportunities ahead to mingle and network. Your confidence and charisma is on the rise, someone notices and is drawn to getting to know you better. It does bring an expansive time of adventure and endless possibilities. It lights up new potential and could lead to a romantic experience with someone quirky and unique. Lively discussions, enticing communication, bring this situation to life. This is someone you meet in a community environment, they have known the complexities of love and romance, and have their own painful story to share. It does reveal a social life which is going to be vibrant, dynamic, and exciting. This person doesn't want to become involved in drama, they have had enough of that in the past, there ready to build foundations which are stable, and progressive. It is a time which resonates warmly, setting positive intentions, sets the right kind of environment. He does trigger happy surprises, and this culminates in a meaningful time. This person treasures developing a bond with you. It is a situation that unfolds gently, drawing joy into your world. You hit a high point with this person; it is a time which brings case closer; a sharing of a particular moment is ahead.

Ideas & Creativity

It is a time of good news and exciting potential. Overall, you find that life flows more efficiently, your situation progresses, and information reaches you, which is seen as a positive step in the right direction. It is a time that triggers change, and as such, it does nourish your aspirations to improve your situation. You discover a more social environment is on offer, and this gives you room to stretch your boundaries. It is a time that sees you being productive, digging for gold, and expanding your horizons. It does have an open road for you to pick and choose the areas which spark your interest the most. Being in sync with your intuition provides you with glittering options to explore. You find yourself in a landscape that creates change, and this touches many areas of your life with new blessings. It does mark the beginning of a process that is built upon.

Issues & Hurdles

The Supermoon in Libra this month provides you with a prime time to release the past, letting go of resentments and frustrations resolves areas that have been holding you back. It is a time that brings endings, transitions, and change. You are wise to do your due diligence and go over your life's path carefully. You are set to benefit from the planning you undertake. It does enable you to focus your attention correctly and feel that your foundations are secure. You can embrace the chapter ahead, it motivates you to push back barriers, release restrictions, and enter uncharted territory. There is good news coming, information arrives to light the way forward. You are making tracks and can soon embrace positive feedback. You have had difficulties along this journey, and you are ready to travel across sunnier skies. An area you reach for does soon blossom. It enables you to make the most of this time, you wrap up a cycle which has been problematic, and can create space for a new flow of energy to tempt you forward. It is a time of progress and planning for the future. You've had some difficulty dealing with life, but it won't be much longer before you cross new skies, which have a sunnier outlook. It is a time which may see you change direction, as you are so ready to become the best version of yourself. Purifying your energy during the Supermoon aids in creating space for the new potential to arrive soon afterward.

MAY HOROSCOPE

ASTROLOGICAL THEME & ZODIAC ENERGY

CENTERED ~ INFLUENTIAL ~ SPIRITED

WORK & CAREER

Out with the old and in with the new! It's full steam ahead, you are ready to embrace a new chapter, things are on the move, it does have you re-evaluating your goals, and choosing an area which is in alignment with your vision. You may shift or change your priorities thinking about the future, does broaden your perspective of what is possible. It's a great time to plant the seeds for future growth. There is a theme emerging in your life which underscores a sense of abundance, which seeks to blossom in your world. It does have you revealing opportunities that arrive to support an active phase of growth. This is the ticket to get the ball rolling on an exciting stage of developing your vision. You're ready to kick off a chapter which is connected to pursuing your goals. You can soon initiate the development of an area that enables you to expand your dreams. Your approach to life is currently evolving, this allows your talents to shine, it leads to a change of mindset, one where you can feel more in control of the direction you are heading towards. Reinventing your situation is the perfect way to bring new energy into play. It does allow you to remove elements that no longer serve your purpose and stay focused on improving your situation by being flexible and adaptable to change.

LOVE & ROMANCE

Couples

This person does see you as someone who inspires their mind. Your love interest feels you are a sensitive person whose imagination is ripe with creative ideas and dreams. They see you as someone sensitive, hardwired to form meaningful bonds. This person thinks that things will unfold over time; they still unsure of goals, but the journey is an essential part of revealing the real potential possible. They do feel open to seeing where it takes you both. You are on the right path to developing a closer bond. This one is a genuinely caring person with a strong work ethic, they see you as someone who has a big heart, and is on a quest to discover what the possibilities hold. Your partner is a practical person who aims high in life and usually succeeds. It's all looking very promising, expanding your horizons, creates the space needed to see this situation flourish.

Singles

A surprise is waiting in your inbox soon. You hear from someone you have been thinking about, and the energy sent out on a vibrational level does get this one thinking about reaching out. It leads to a lively discussion where you catch up and share recent events. It could spark the outpouring of pent up emotions, it allows the situation to flow forward, this person is ready to open their heart and begin a new chapter. News reaches you, which has traveled quite a long way. It does see someone from the past re-emerging in your life. Taking time to process and integrate this surprise, does restore equilibrium, as this person resurfaces, old sensitivities can also soon crop up. However, reconnecting with this person leads to an unexpected opportunity to heal the past. You have likely crossed his path previously, a reconnection sees things moving in a more positive direction. This person has a strong influence over your emotions during the chapter head. It does see a social gathering which draws you both together. It is profoundly transformational and leads to a thoroughly personal bond flourishing. This brings excitement and adventure bursting into your world.

IDEAS & CREATIVITY

You have a knack for revealing hidden information. It does give you a broader perspective, seeing the full picture, enables you to shift your focus towards an avenue which offers you room to grow your situation. You may find that your imagination is sparking with new inspiration soon, this has you dreaming big about a future goal. Expect further information to cross your path soon. Opportunity comes knocking soon, it does enable you to feel inspired about life as things are on the upswing. You have a gorgeous ability to make the most of refreshing options that tempt you towards expanding your consciousness. It is a beautiful theme that offers you a chance to embark on a new chapter. As you improve your circumstances, you initiate an active phase of growth.

Issues & Hurdles

You have been through an unsettling time, and as you've been dealing with a lot lately, take time to nurture your spirit, focus on your path, your journey. This is a time where you can release the past and remove areas that limit progress. It does enable you to transition forwards and seek a chapter that is more in alignment with the person you are currently becoming. Life holds a refreshing change soon. While you have known stormy weather, your ability to overcome hurdles and reach the other side does enable you to make the most of the changes, which have swirled into your life. It is a time that draws movement, discovery, and new experiences. Broadening your perception enables you to spot an area worth developing. Things may feel up in the air at this time, and that is okay. Don't stress about your situation, you are going to soon land in a landscape which is more stable, secure, and balanced. You have been through a significant time of growing your soul and can continue to focus on areas that nourish your spirit. There is much to look forward to ahead, an opportunity arrives which supports your vision.

JUNE HOROSCOPE

Astrological Theme & Zodiac Energy

Effective ~ Efficient ~ Adaptable

Work & Career

There are some upcoming changes which offer you room to grow your situation. A goal that you have been seeking begins to take shape, your determination enables you to pursue your dream. With a few tweaks, you can effectively make progress on obtaining this area. It does see life becoming smoother and more comfortable to navigate, security is on the rise. A situation you nurture is set to take off like a firecracker in the weeks to come. It sees life come full circle, you're likely to have signs and clues that something unusual is ready to kick into your life. As you transition forward, you get a scope on an area which offers room to progress. You reveal a region that holds interest; it provides you an auspicious chapter. Information arrives, which brings terrific news. It leads to an upcoming project and does give you something inspiring to sink your teeth into. Taking special note of the report, you receive leads to brainstorming with friends. There is good news about a venture which offers you room to grow your talents. It does enable you to progress a broader goal of drawing more security into your life. There is a social aspect that puts you in contact with others of a similar mindset; it heightens career potential.

Love & Romance

Couples

A refreshing change is coming; this opens the potential for a more stable bond to emerge. Taking a long-term approach is going to give you the best chance of success. Allowing this to unfurl gently over time, without trying to force the connection forward, helps process changing emotional foundations. This person feels encouraged to nurture the bond gently, this is a good thing. It sees a situation changing and evolving, this has you moving in the right direction. It does give you opportunities to deepen the case, and it leads to ideas which nurture your vision. The right type of energy flows into your world, this helps you enter a cycle where you can accomplish more growth. The icing on the cake is when a discussion takes place, which is spoken directly from the heart.

Singles

It is the time of social expansion, invitations arrive to support a phase of growth. Mingling and networking, you discover a person with impeccable taste and integrity, this is someone who has high standards, this person is charming, gracious, and magnetic. They are a witty individual with a natural flair for making you feel comfortable. This person has a winning way of connecting with you, it does open your eyes to the potential possible. You connect with a person who is dynamic, self-assured, confident, and charismatic. This person has a way of speaking, which paints a picture, their vivid imagination, and style with words lead to lively discussions. This is someone who loves traveling and getting involved in learning about different cultures. Their manner is purposeful, creative, and warm. It does set the stage for a bond to be nurtured. This person wants to know you, they are keeping their eyes open for the right environment to build a better experience with you. It does seem a lot will be happening in your social life, this leads to a time of transformation and rejuvenation, it does help you push barriers back and move forward towards developing a situation which leaves you feeling enthusiastic about future possibilities. This person's energy is magnetic.

IDEAS & CREATIVITY

It is a time of change, it offers you a fresh start, potential arrives to stoke the fires of your inspiration. It is a time of growth and progression, you create a shift forward, and this sees things picking up speed. The conditions are right to grow your vision. Laying the groundwork builds stable foundations, and this provides you with the right environment to advance your life. It is a different time that adds the spice of excitement to your world. Necessary changes occur, which enable growth to become smoother, it does see you moving forward, the floodgates open, and you are excited about how things unfold in the months ahead. You hear good news, and this inspires your mind; it has you set goals that are long term and ambitious. Having aspirations to work towards does put you in manifestation mode, it enables things to come together nicely. You get a better idea of the direction ahead, and this builds more stable foundations, it could lead to a significant win, as a goal you have in mind comes together.

You discover a situation blossoms under a landscape of shared goals and aspirations. You also see results from a position which is nurtured, it does draw a sweet aspect into your life, and this blends beautifully with your hopes for a brighter future. There are opportunities to connect with intuition and creativity ahead; this will help you tune into the signs, which do run through your life.

Issues & Hurdles

You have been through a hard time, it has been unsettling, yet led to a great deal of personal growth. Understanding your needs on a deeper level provides the path for a glorious chapter, which is magnificent. It does place emphasis on developing your goals, and this is a trend that continues over the coming months. You land in a landscape that offers room to grow your creative side. News reaches you, which have you considering the path ahead. It is a time where you discover deeper truths about yourself and the situations you need in your life. It is a time which has you seek out social events and supportive friends. It does suggest you attend a gathering which enables you to share thoughts with others who are on the same page. The atmosphere is rejuvenating and good for your soul. The more you think about your goals, the more it takes you towards developing this situation. It does lead to a time of building stable foundations and gently moving forward towards a brighter chapter. It is a time of removing limitations, releasing outworn energy, and healing the past. It does create the space for new chapter potential to flow into your world, and this guides you towards a path of abundance.

JULY HOROSCOPE

ASTROLOGICAL THEME & ZODIAC ENERGY

COURAGEOUS ~ DIRECTED ~ ADVENTUROUS

WORK & CAREER

Mercury retrograde ends on July 12th, the time is now ripe to go after your goals. Trusting the universe to support your expansion, you can take flight and seek a path that draws abundance into your life. Essential new information crosses your path soon, it does enable you to set foot on solid ground, you contemplate your goals, and gain a remarkable vision of what can be achieved over the coming months. It is a time of careful planning and the projection of a concept that inspires your mind. You point the way forward towards a journey which is paved with glittering options. You are also naturally innovative, progressive, and creative. You turn a corner soon, your willingness to seek out new prospects, leads to tangible results. Your quick thinking mind uncovers a path that offers you room to grow your situation. You can plot a course towards the achievement of your goals; things are on the move soon. The work you undertake continues to better your situation. It lands you in a prosperous cycle. It does draw substantial changes that drive your progress towards ever-larger goals. This does have you refining and evaluating your purposes, so you can make the most of the opportunities which arrive to tempt your situation forward. It is a vivid and dynamic time that brings forward-moving options.

LOVE & ROMANCE

Couples

Information is revealed for the Cancerian in a relationship, this occurs at or soon after the Lunar Eclipse on July 5th, it gives you clarity about the situation with your love interest and with the end of the Mercury Retrograde phase this month, your romantic location is set to blossom, you enter an exciting time, which sets the stage for growth to occur in your personal life. It does see you headed towards a happy chapter, forging ahead, you begin to see progress happening, this inspires and motivates. It does draw activities that are suitable for your soul. A meaningful moment gives you the sign you have been seeking. It is a green light event, enabling you to feel you are gaining traction on your vision. It is an essential time, it helps you feel more confident about developing this situation. It does draw an opportunity to bring a close connection to life. You embrace the increased stability, it enables you to feel that this is worth your time. Something special is brewing. Overall, there is a desire to build a better bold and take the time necessary to improve communication. It's not a linear progression; this person does need time to re-balance energy, as they have many demands on his time, which can drain energy. It can leave you wondering where you stand. Being patient, allowing them time to come to you, does lead this person to trust in this process.

Singles

This month does offer some exciting options to get the ball rolling on a new chapter in romance. You unwrap a phase that sparks with outings, activities, and other creative adventures. It does draw a new situation, this dramatically shifts your focus towards developing a bond. This someone feels unique, they have an intriguing style. Spending time getting to know this person leaves you wanting more. A secret is revealed when someone shares their more profound thoughts. It does push you towards a phase of expansion, you see a new situation blossom. This shines a light on developing a bond with one who captures your interest. Spending time in a social environment is right for your soul, it gives you plenty to celebrate. There are signs that this is going to move into new territory soon. You connect with a charismatic and dedicated person who has a sophistical and gracious approach to life. This is someone who aims high in life and usually succeeds. They are steadfast, dependable, and reliable. It does drive a situation forward, you discover a desire to embrace a new chapter of potential with the one who draws excitement into your world. Embarking on developing this situation lets your head down, it brings freedom into your life.

IDEAS & CREATIVITY

A lunar eclipse combines with the full moon in Capricorn. This is the Wolf Moon, it may feel like an unsettling time where there have been many rapid changes, things are now headed towards a new path, it does bring you an enticing option. Some curious changes are occurring for you soon, you may quickly discover a way which sparkles with potential. It is a time where you explore uncharted territory and create a landscape speckled with enticing new options. You reach a milestone soon, which helps you map out future goals. It is a time of fanciful dreaming, you set your sights on goals that feel out of reach, but you would be surprised at the growth you can obtain if you focus your attention on achieving your vision. Your resourcefulness provides you with a path towards successful outcomes. It leads to a more secure chapter, it provides you with the stability you need, it brings the foundations necessary to grow your life. In fact, it's the start of something big for you, it gives you the ability to flex your wings and expand your life in areas that bring joy. There is a shift forward for you soon, it's the fresh start you have been hoping for. It brings with it a broader vista of new possibilities. It does have you feeling motivated and inspired to explore new territory. Life becomes brighter, as greener pastures beckon, this takes the situation forward and advances your goals. It does have you putting together a plan which offers room to grow your life.

Issues & Hurdles

Saturn makes an entrance on July 20th, this coincides with the new Moon in Cancer. The energy of the past is coming up, this enables you to reflect on what has gone before, it can bring up sensitive emotions, this is part of the healing process, it improves the stability possible in your world by enabling you time to process difficult emotions, and resolve outworn energy. You can move away from areas which have disappointed you in the past. Moving into unseen waters may feel unsettling, yet draws fantastic options to light. It does demonstrate your ability to take the plunge and make the most of what you discover. You are ready to reap the rewards of a new chapter. Taking time to focus on your vision draws the right situation. Having faith that things are going to move forward correctly is essential. It enables you to trust in the process of developing your life and expanding your horizons. As you push back barriers, you can dive into new territory, and know that you are supported during this phase of steady growth. Further information arrives soon, it gives you a unique insight into the path ahead. This is valuable information, and it does bring with it the currency inspiration.

AUGUST HOROSCOPE

ASTROLOGICAL THEME & ZODIAC ENERGY

GIVING ~ NOBLE ~ COURAGEOUS

WORK & CAREER

It is a time that brings gifts and luck; you enter a phase that gives you the green light to obtain your career goals. It does take a few weeks to come together, which culminates in a new role being started early in the new year. It is a riveting time which sees your situation improving, you have an open road of growth ahead. It does bring stability and security into your world, this releases the pressure, and advances your situation. It is a busy time that focuses on developing your goals. You hear exciting news about a career option; it does bring trustworthy information which captures your attention and enables you to plot a course forward. There are also options to mingle, which see you spending time with group activities. It is a sweet month to improve your social life, the chances of finding a romance significantly enhance. It is a time which sets in motion new options, it is a freedom-loving chapter, you find the courage to free yourself from restrictions, and this sees your life becoming exceptionally busy with new opportunities. You are ready to embrace a new flow of potential, it does lead to impressive results as your ability to improve your situation is skyrocketing.

LOVE & ROMANCE

Couples

You see an improvement in your home situation, your emotional security is on the rise, and this draws an energizing chapter where you can explore the possibilities with someone who inspires your heart. It does lead to meaningful conversations and new plans. Looking within opens a powerful window of insight, it enables you to review the past, you may come up with a refreshing new outlook on the situation. It is an area that has left you feeling vulnerable and raw, but it is an especially good time to release complicated feelings, as more communication is likely to occur at some stage moving forward, and being in the right frame of mind will get the next chapter off to the best start.

Singles

This is a time which is going to bring you in contact with a variety of people, it does bring new leads, you enter an expansive time which sees you lucky in love. Meeting someone who turns out to be worth your time, has you feeling inspired about the potential possible. It reinvents your life, inspiring change. Staying open to new potential does bring an exciting chapter. Someone curious enters your world, this person is sensitive, compassionate, and most importantly, flexible. They have been going through a time of transition themselves, they understand your situation. This is someone intuitive, a person who draws abundance into your world. It does see a new adventure occurring in your personal life.

IDEAS & CREATIVITY

You are the recipient of welcome news soon, it leaves you feeling inspired, your head is free and clear, taking advantage of new opportunities, does bring you to a bright and beautiful place. It does see good luck swirling around you, it leads to a more creative chapter, one where you can focus on a personal passion, and develop it into something incredible. You are ready to create change, planning is instrumental, plot a course, set your destination in your intuitive GPS, and take the action steps necessary to see your dreams to fruition. You uncover a bounty of possibilities, it does know the goodness begins to flow into your life. The energy which refreshes and rejuvenates heightens your optimism and does give you the boost required to put your can-do attitude into play. You have a good reason to look forward to the month ahead. It does see support flowing into your world, is the perfect time to be out and circulating with your friends. See what the world has to offer, and you discover a pleasing situation. It might surprise you, as it provides you a chance to tear off in a new direction. It is a time that brings fantastic news; it sets the stage for an exciting chapter.

ISSUES & HURDLES

You discover things come together when the timing is suitable to progress your life path further. It is a time of waiting for news, the erratic vibrations surrounding this situation does lead to things being up in the air. Currently, it is a time of watching and waiting for new information. As you journey through the darkness, you walk a well-worn trail towards the light. You are a pilgrim on a journey to develop your world and discover your higher calling. Being mindful of the complexities which surround your situation enables you to progress forward in a balanced and sustainable manner. The hidden information is also coming, which illuminates a path ahead. Some of your biggest obstacles are self-imposed, the limitations you set on yourself can hold you back from achieving your highest result. Working on dissolving blockages, healing the past, and removing outworn energies, all light a path towards a new chapter of abundance. It does take your situation forward, and this kicks off a section of happiness and growth. You are facing a crossroads, it does see information being revealed soon, which help you make a firm decision. This does offer you a path that draws more abundance into your world. It is the first step of a powerful journey.

SEPTEMBER HOROSCOPE

ASTROLOGICAL THEME & ZODIAC ENERGY

CALMING ~ DEPENDABLE ~ UNDERSTANDING

WORK & CAREER

A decision made at this time does crack open the potential possible. In short, it opens a gateway, and this sees fresh opportunity flow into your working life. It does take perseverance and a willingness to practice and learn the knowledge you have acquired thoroughly. Your career goals come into focus, and creating a strategic plan enables you to navigate the complexities using a tenacious and determined outlook. You gain assistance from a mentor who offers to guide you through this process. It does see you going from strength to strength and obtaining this goal. It is a time that focuses on taking your situation to new heights. You are drawn to developing your vision, and it does show a blessing coming into your world. Your focus is on increasing stability and security; it sees a substantial goal coming into focus, which enables you to shift your situation forward. As you advance your circumstances, you incorporate new options that expand the potential possible. Success is written all over the chapter head. As you lift the shutters on areas that have limited progress, you see positive signs that much is possible in the chapter ahead. It does directly align you towards advancement, this is a time of development where you can accomplish a robust result. It has you feeling proud and inspired.

LOVE & ROMANCE

Couples

Life moves forward splendidly, it is a time of catching up, sharing profound conversations, and shifting the focus to planning for future events. It does connect you with your love interest on a deeper level, this person appreciates your support, and is looking forward to sharing ideas and thoughts with you. They feel ready to advance this situation, this is giving them the confidence needed to step out of their usual comfort zone. This person is sincere and transparent with you. They feel you both share an excellent rapport, and it feels comfortable bonding with you. It's going to be an excellent chapter, which leads to moments you can treasure. You reveal a closer bond is possible; it offers a sense of abundance which has future possibilities are written all over it.

Singles

You are in a time of transition, one cycle has ended, and another is just beginning to emerge. There are sparks ready to be ignited, focusing your energy in this direction, does plant the seeds which blossom over time. Following your heart, moving in alignment with your vision, you discover this situation becomes closer, foundations are built which enable progress to occur over time. The energy is active and dynamic, and this makes it susceptible to change over time. You discover you can build a closer bond, it does enable you to feel the depth of connection with this person. It corresponds with a lovely path that draws abundance, and you could easily see the romantic overtones ignite into something tangible in your world. This person does find you enticing, they feel you have a creative flair and an imaginative outlook. This person is a sincere individual with a strong sense of self. They can appear light-hearted and casual, but they have a mysterious depth, which is only revealed once you get past their initial barriers. This person is a positive thinker and does feel you are someone who has a similar trait.

IDEAS & CREATIVITY

You reveal information which enlightens and inspires. This news is symbolic of a higher spiritual calling, which is emerging in your life. It leads to a path that is enchanting, eclectic, and diverse. You can harness innovative, creative, and trailblazing energy to forge a path towards your higher spiritual goals. It does resonate with a wonderfully abundant gateway towards a brighter future. There is a change of setting for you, one which rejuvenates and renews your spirit. It does place a strong emphasis on personal growth. A rare opportunity may light the path forward, this spreads a sparkling wildfire of potential through your life ahead. Magic and mayhem arrive to draw you towards new adventures. It does require an open heart and a willingness to explore uncharted territory. You have a tremendous capacity for compassion, honoring your gifts enables you to share your vision of empathy and idealism. It does pave the way to grow your world exponentially. It places the spotlight on improving your life through your ability to also help others. Your dedication and perseverance enable you to develop a vision that is inspiring. It does illuminate a path of transformation ahead. This leads to a happier chapter. It is a phase of reinvention, creating change inspires your mind, and this gives you an open path to explore, as exciting new adventures soon call your name.

ISSUES & HURDLES

A reminder of the past evokes a sharp memory, this nostalgic and sentimental trip down memory lane has actually occurred as a form of synchronicity. It is guiding you towards healing and closure, it helps you shut the door on a problematic area, and you know instinctively that this is the correct course. Once you create space to heal what never eventuated, a shift forward draws new options. You have been through an unsettling time where there have been many rapid changes, things are now headed towards an original path. In fact, you can soon reach a turning point and ultimately release the hold that the past has on you, this actually creates space for releasing all that stands in the way between you and your happiness. You are set to blaze through a time which is more self-expressive, and joyful. The past has been an incredible time of learning, and this has strengthened your spirit as you have overcome many hurdles and come out the other side better for having made progress, even under challenging times. It does now take you to a crossroads, you have a chance to explore an area which offers you room to grow your vision further. It is a beautiful time of contemplating the path ahead, drawing abundance into your life.

OCTOBER HOROSCOPE

ASTROLOGICAL THEME & ZODIAC ENERGY

RESPONSIBLE ~ PROFOUND ~ DEDICATED

WORK & CAREER

News is imminent, which sees you make lovely progress on achieving an elevated career pathway. It ushers a new chapter into your life, it does see you working in a new environment. It's a great time to clear the decks in preparation for this new role. You will be moving to an area that takes in new adventures, and this transition enables you to advance your situation and achieve growth and security. It will be this job or another one soon. You should expect the unexpected, a message is coming, this news is unusual, but it offers you a chance to expand your life and obtain a new level of growth. It highlights a path of fulfillment and contentment. Vibrant outcomes are possible through a willingness to expand your horizons into new areas. An offer is coming up soon. It draws upon your lucrative talents, it's an area which harnesses your innate abilities, and really enables you to shine. It does see you advancing your situation, as it does have success written all over it. It allows you to shift your focus forwards and begin to dream big about the possibilities. Things are on track to progress your life. What you may not see the complete picture yet, it does reveal a chapter ahead which draws new options to light. A shift occurs, which offers you a robust area to develop; it kicks off grander plans and even connects you with a fabulous goal. You do see growth which draws positive energy into your world. It opens a gateway to a future that can be expanded upon.

LOVE & ROMANCE

Couples

This person contributes many gifts to the situation, they will make sure you feel comfortable and at home within the case. It does see communication being a vital part of developing this bond, it leads to an expansive chapter, many gifts are set to unfold. Your thoughtfulness will be appreciated, your gestures won't go unnoticed, it does secure a more stable foundation with this person. He feels that your support is vital, it does give him a positive sign that this is a prospect that can be developed. If things have been stalling recently, this is a beautiful way to shift the focus forward, and change things up with him. It resonates with an excellent ripple effect of abundance, this person pays it forward to you. It is a situation which is likely to pick up speed over the coming weeks, as the bond deepens, there is plenty to be excited about. You enter a more active phase of planning for future growth. It does see opportunities arrive with this person, and you can embrace a more connected situation.

Singles

Mercury Retrograde delivers a bump in the road when it arrives on the 13th; you can navigate around it by being flexible. While Mercury Retrograde sees you reflecting on a situation that has left you feeling nostalgic, this contemplation allows you to gain a better understanding of how past events have brought you to this crossroads. A decision ahead does draw new options into your romantic life. There is a hive of activity ahead, you make strides in this busy and active environment. It is a bustle, and this is the perfect time to embrace a more social vibe, it draws new friendships to light, bringing a gift of companionship. There is a fresh wind blowing into your life soon. It leads to an active phase where you can progress your personal goals. You feel inspired to scale back your schedule and focus your energy on an area that draws harmony into your life. It does lead to a more social environment, you discover communication flows effortlessly with a kindred spirit. This person inspires your mind, a flight of fancy takes place, and this inspires you to dive into new territory.

IDEAS & CREATIVITY

You transition towards a significant event which is positive, but difficult in the short term. Mercury Retrogrades appearance creates a shift which requires strength, and fortitude. However, this blessing in disguise leads to a glorious outcome, you do discover a richly abundant path, heighten opportunities light a new journey forward. As the veil between worlds is thinning this month, you can notice more signs from spirit; it is an ideal opportunity to connect with those who have crossed over. Some curious changes are coming up for you, it does see you guided towards an emotionally rewarding area. Your intuition is heightened, this lets you become more perceptive and sensitive to signs which guide your path forward. It is a wonderfully social time, which sees new energy flowing into your world. It is a time which is ripe with promise and potential. Setting positive intentions is the first step in realizing your goals. It's also important to release expectations and enable the universe to work its magic in the background. It's going to take a little longer for things to come together, but there's a glorious chance you see tangible progress soon. It does draw an energizing time, which leaves you feeling especially uplifted and optimistic.

ISSUES & HURDLES

There is a need for patience, balance, and perspective this month. It is essential to allow time for your creative ideas to germinate in the womb of your consciousness. Don't try to force or rush positive change in your life during the Mercury Retrograde phase, but gently guide this process forward. It can be valuable to create space to process your emotions and rebuild an environment that heals and re-calibrates your spirit. This helps you turn that corner and shift towards a happier chapter. There will soon be time to rest and unwind and process those denser emotions you have been dealing with this year. You may feel under pressure, and needed time to re-balance flagging energy. It's as if you are juggling many balls, trying to keep everything together, and not knowing indeed where your heart is at. It does see life becoming lighter, it draws a path which sparkles with good fortune and advancement. Creating space to rediscover life in a new manner, does light a way forward. You are a fighter, you have an incredible ability to persevere and come out on top. No matter what happens in life, you have the capabilities to come up with some pretty ingenious solutions. You may be in the market to expand your life, and this open spirit creates space for something enterprising to arrive, it flings open the doors to a new chapter.

NOVEMBER HOROSCOPE

Astrological Theme & Zodiac Energy

Curious ~ Energetic ~ Visionary

Work & Career

Information is coming, which sparks your curiosity, it does see the new potential is set to blossom in your life. It is a time that drives your talents further as you embark on developing a passion project which offers room to grow your skills. It is a month of movement and discovery for you at work, which involves either traveling, new projects, or the developing of fresh ideas. You are ready to move forward in your career, and this month ushers in increased communications, as it enables creative dialogue with a mentor. This will help develop your concepts to the next level. Through this communication, you find inspirational insight which leaves you feeling confident and optimistic that you are going in the right direction. This is a perfect month to use focused powers of analysis, and create brilliant ideas that illuminate the path ahead in your career. There are changes ahead for you at work as you see the culmination of an undertaking completed. You are ready to complete this process and forge ahead on your own. This undertaking can even represent moving away from your current workplace and finding a new position that meets your current career goals. There is a need to remove outworn energy and move forward on your own with originality, innovation, and rejuvenation. This is about finding your place in the world, transforming your life, and following your chosen path. This is a time which provides hidden gems, it sees your success rate flourish, as you blaze a trail towards achieving your dreams.

Love & Romance

Couples

You may have some emotional intensity surrounding the situation; perhaps doubt has crept into your mind; it is a situation which does best when nurtured, focusing attention on developing this bond, enables it to grow and deepen without distraction. It sees the situation becoming more balanced, the foundations are stable and able to grow and flourish. There opportunities ahead that give you positive signs that you are on the path. It does seem a situation taking off in due course. Taking a moment at this time to recalibrate your energy, enables you to create stability, and prepare to embrace a fresh chapter of potential. There is a situation which comes knocking, it has your heart feeling excited, meaningful conversations, lead to a deep, bonded situation. Focusing on this person creates a mood for romance and excitement. You can put your goals front and center, focusing on achieving your dreams, fast-tracks your situation towards personal growth. It does move out of your comfort zone, into new territory, and awakening to the bounty which tempts you forward, you walk in alignment with your spirit, with one who captures your imagination. It takes you upstream towards a meaningful chapter of romance and excitement.

Singles

It is time that may see you feeling lucky in love. It brings a bold push forward on your path, a thrilling encounter might arrive unexpectedly, and you will be glad that you didn't settle for just anyone. It does see a situation blossoming suddenly and swiftly, you get a confidence boost when admirer shares their thoughts with you. It does see you aligning with the one who makes your heart sing. There are lovely indications that this situation is set to develop further. You mark a milestone with this person, it brings a memorable moment, a meaningful gift is likely to cross your path. It is a fantastic chapter that sees you touching down on a closer bond. Things come together nicely. You are headed towards a busy time that offers social expansion. Being willing to dive into uncharted territory does bring dividends. You make headway on your goals, it opens a new chapter around your personal life. This person is sensitive, they are at home being intimate and having quiet getaways, as they enjoy developing and nurturing the bond. This is not someone who needs a crowd around them.

IDEAS & CREATIVITY

Something new is on the way for you; there is a creative element that blends perfectly with your artistic side. This month looks at all your creative energy as you distill it down, refining the potential, to end up with the highest primary fuel possible. This is achieved by stilling your mind and rebalancing your energy. Allow passion to ignite your inspiration, and use this furnace to develop your creativity to higher levels. Synthesis and refinement will transform your current potential towards higher achievement. As you refine this energy, ask yourself what the profound significance of this potential is, and objectively evaluate the answers that come to you. Symbolism is rife in your life, and accurately understanding its meaning will allow you to continue to fine-tune this potential to bring into physical reality, new and higher energy that has not yet been experienced thus far. This process of purification gives you the power to eliminate old outworn belief structures that have been hindering your progress. It allows you to create potent alchemy where you harness all elements with precise measurements, to create a recipe for success. It is a magical time, it leaves you feeling inspired and creative, it draws you towards an appreciation of simple joys. This is a month which inspires you and characterizes an abundance of creative enthusiasm. You are encouraged to engage in creative undertakings, and you express a willingness to try new things. Your encounters, endeavors, and creative pursuits this month will be pleasurable and satisfying.

ISSUES & HURDLES

The problematic energy eases as Mercury Retrograde ends on the 3rd. Your strength and fortitude are the backbones of your family. Tending to obligations keeps you busy, but it's also essential to facilitate between bursts of energy by creating space where you can rest and escape into a creative cocoon. Don't become overburdened with responsibilities, prioritize your own well-being, and this will nurture your spirit in ways that you cannot currently understand. All in all, it is a time that draws a sentimental theme into your world. As you revisit a previous chapter, you can appreciate how far you have traveled on your journey. It gives you the ability to broaden your perspective, this changes everything, it enables you to plot a course towards future goals. You're at a crossroads, but do not fear change, things are not going to be as difficult as you fear, you are being guided to stay open to new options and they are going to be flowing into your life soon. Now is the time to clear the decks, to create the space necessary and to broaden your view of what is possible. You soon awaken a wonderful sense of creativity which inspires growth. You are courageous, a real pillar of strength to those around you. This is a time where you mingle with your wider circle of friends, you can take advantage of these opportunities to socialize, as it enables you a sense of rejuvenation, it places a strong focus on friendships and collaborations which hold meaning. Putting yourself out there is the way to go.

DECEMBER HOROSCOPE

ASTROLOGICAL THEME & ZODIAC ENERGY

DYNAMIC ~ GENEROUS ~ ORIGINAL

WORK & CAREER

You are entering a vital time relating to your career path. It does suggest a professional opportunity is arriving soon, this gives you a fantastic reward for the work you have undertaken this year. This is a time that represents new beginnings, opportunities, and potential. It is a time of completion, from which you finish one part of your work life and you begin a new phase in your career. Like the burst of spring after the long winter, you are ready for a new beginning as a fresh vision enters your awareness. Renewal is forecast on many levels for you this month. As you stand at the threshold of a new phase in your work life and career, you are ready to go through the gateway of transformation. Your creative vision, emotional, intellectual, and physical condition is transforming towards new horizons. Great leaps of faith lead to dramatic change. You now have the energy and courage to cross over this threshold, and emerge into a new phase of working life. This impacts your life on many levels. An unexpected opportunity may come your way, and this gives you something to feel inspired about. It opens your horizons, and takes you to a chapter of exciting adventures.

LOVE & ROMANCE

Couples

Things are on the move, you begin to focus on planning for future events, it's time which sees miracles happening. It is an optimistic chapter that holds the promise of sunny skies. You head towards a culmination of sorts, an event you attend has the air of celebration, it does spark with new energy. You dive forward towards advancement in your personal life and are finally able to set your sights on a lofty goal. A revelation is revealed, leading to a breakthrough. This information marks a time where you understand the past on a deeper level. It does see decisive action taking you towards committing to a new chapter. Necessary changes occur, which sees new beginnings being possible, it does see you on a journey of advancing your situation. Cracking open fresh goals, you are ready to reap the rewards of progressing your case. It is connected with expansion in your social life, you draw new friendships, and invitations out leave you feeling inspired. In fact, it's a golden time to transform your life and create space to nurture your world. You are given the green light to embrace a highly connected time ahead.

Singles

A friend shares a secret with you soon; this reveals a profound attraction. It is headline news, it comes a surprise, yet it does offer you a chance to develop a deeper bond. Enjoying close talks with this person gives you a new perspective of the potential possible. It does see you making progress on your personal life, and leaves you feeling positive about making the changes necessary to obtain your goals. This person does feel attracted to you, they are willing to tackle their dreams and take things up a notch. They are looking for the right time to cross that line and share their thoughts with you. This person is someone who enjoys spice and excitement, they are spontaneous and may just surprise you with an out of the blue conversation. It does provide the framework for a more connected situation with this individual. This is someone who does feel there is a spark of chemistry between you both. It does suggest that they are looking for the right time to improve the connection and see what grows. They have been through a time of uncertainty, and are now wanting to build more stable foundations. It does mark a time that sees your focus shifting forward; it translates to a closer bond that gently unfurls over time.

IDEAS & CREATIVITY

December is a month that provides you with heightened creative powers. You are ready to pull the trigger and unleash a new chapter into your world. You bring structure to the transient and intangible this month. Driven by strong, idealistic beliefs, you seek to establish a firm foundation and secure a fundamental basis for future growth. Use creative skills to organize, coordinate, and create your own empire. By developing these structured ideas, you achieve stability, security, and liberation. You are creatively inspired, encouraging, and courageous of heart. Leadership abilities come out and enable you to shine, you easily balance conflicts, and harness your fighting spirit to draw magic energy to you, allowing you to overflow with confidence. Taking control of situations, you forge a path forward with a focused and determined mind. You make creative and inspired plans, set boundaries, and look at things differently to find the way to move past obstacles with excitement, as you captivate your enthusiasm and obtain tangible results.

ISSUES & HURDLES

There is an undercurrent of transformation occurring in your life, the year is complete, it has been eventful, it has been a journey into growth and learning. You may find yourself troubled by a restless spirit as you question your place in the world this month. You are looking for positive feedback from the Universe, that you are on the right path to achieving your goals. Your dreams often can appear tantalizingly just out of reach, making you question if you are headed in the right direction. Ask the divine for guidance and signs of communication, will help guide your emotional and intuitive outlook. The mysterious energy you feel around you at night is igniting the vast sea of possibilities open to you. This can appear confusing, and lead to feelings of doubt. Trust and develop a faith that you are being guided towards spiritual truth. A clear picture of what you are destined to achieve will soon emerge to guide you. You are given space during the solstice on the 21st to reflect on the difficulties you have faced, and how you rebalanced your emotions, you find that life you can better control your feelings and accept what life throws at you without becoming destabilized. An emotionally balanced and calm approach enables you to face challenges head-on. It is a time of rest and renewal for you, as you have been over exerting yourself on emotional levels, and there is a need to replenish your inner resources to rebalance emotions. Taking time out to reflect and rebuild your energy is needed this month. Engage in relaxing activities, meditation, and other peaceful pursuits. This will help you merge your emotional landscape with your passions, and allow your energy to become more grounded, stable, and balanced.

ASTROLOGICAL DIARY

2020

Astrological Diary

2020

Time is set to Coordinated Universal Time Zone (UT±0)

January

Mon 30

Tues 31

Wed 1
New Year's Day

Thurs 2

January

Fri 3
First Quarter Moon in Aries. 4.45 UTC
Quadrantids Meteor Shower. Jan 1st-5th. Peaks night of Jan 3rd.

Sat 4

Sun 5

Notes
Lucky Numbers: 11, 62, 12, 61, 32, 5
Astrological Energy: Experiential
Color: White

January

Mon 6

Tues 7

Wed 8

Thurs 9

January

Fri 10
Full Moon in Cancer. Wolf Moon. 19:21 UTC
Penumbral Lunar Eclipse.

Sat 11

Sun 12

Notes
Lucky Numbers: 23, 30, 22, 15, 27, 11
Astrological Energy: Directed
Color: Bone

January

Mon 13

Tues 14

Wed 15

Thurs 16

January

Fri 17

Last Quarter Moon in Libra. 12.58 UTC

Sat 18

Sun 19

Notes

Lucky Numbers: 32, 88, 26, 40, 92, 85
Astrological Energy: Optimistic
Color: Sky Blue

January

Mon 20
Martin Luther King Day

Tues 21

Wed 22

Thurs 23

January

Fri 24
New Moon in Capricorn. 21:42 UTC

Sat 25
Chinese New Year (Rat)

Sun 26
Last Quarter Moon in Scorpio. 21.10 UTC

Notes
Lucky Numbers: 27, 95, 10, 77, 23, 2
Astrological Energy: Visionary
Color: Indigo

January

Mon 27

Tues 28

Weds 29

Thurs 30

January/February

Fri 31

Sat 1
Imbolc

Sun 2
First Quarter Moon in Taurus. 1.42 UTC.
Groundhog Day

Notes
Lucky Numbers: 80, 11, 88, 22, 68, 99
Astrological Energy: Influential
Color: Violet

February

Mon 3

Tues 4

Weds 5

Thurs 6

February

Fri 7

Sat 8

Sun 9
Full Moon in Leo, Supermoon. Snow Moon. 7:33 UTC

Notes
Lucky Numbers: 31, 16, 96, 44, 21, 26
Astrological Energy: Commanding
Color: Midnight Blue

February

Mon 10

Mercury at largest Eastern Elongation.

Tues 11

Weds 12

Thurs 13

February

Fri 14
Valentine's Day

Sat 15
Last Quarter Moon in Scorpio. 22.17 UTC

Sun 16

Notes
Lucky Numbers: 93, 70, 24, 17, 39, 52
Astrological Energy: Imaginative
Color: Royal Blue

February

Mon 17
Presidents' Day

Tues 18
Mercury Retrograde begins

Weds 19

Thurs 20

February

Fri 21

Sat 22

Sun 23
New Moon in Aquarius. 15:32 UTC

Notes
Lucky Numbers: 49, 52, 8, 43, 85, 76
Astrological Energy: Adventurous
Color: Gold

February

Mon 24

Tues 25
Shrove Tuesday (Mardi Gras)

Weds 26
Ash Wednesday

Thurs 27

February/March

Fri 28

Sat 29

Sun 1

Notes

Lucky Numbers: 24, 67, 64, 94, 96, 55
Astrological Energy: Vivacious
Color: Yellow

March

Mon 2

First Quarter Moon in Gemini. 19.57 UTC

Tues 3

Weds 4

Thurs 5

March

Fri 6

Sat 7

Sun 8

Notes

Lucky Numbers: 84, 50, 93, 9, 48, 8
Astrological Energy: Productive
Color: Hot Pink

March

Mon 9
Full Moon in Virgo, Supermoon. Worm Moon. 17:48 UTC
Mercury Retrograde ends.
Purim (begins at sundown)

Tues 10
Purim (ends at sundown)

Weds 11

Thurs 12

March

Fri 13

Sat 14

Sun 15

Notes

Lucky Numbers: 27, 62, 37, 49, 90, 69
Astrological Energy: Passionate
Color: Cyan

March

Mon 16
Last Quarter Moon in Sagittarius. 9.34 UTC

Tues 17
St Patrick's Day

Wed 18

Thurs 19

March

Fri 20
Ostara/Spring Equinox. 3:50 UTC

Sat 21

Sun 22

Notes
Lucky Numbers: 74, 38, 95, 88, 2, 72
Astrological Energy: Constructive
Color: Spring Green

March

Mon 23

Tues 24
Mercury at most substantial Western Elongation.
Venus at most substantial Eastern Elongation.
New Moon in Aries. 9:28 UTC

Weds 25

Thurs 26

March

Fri 27

Sat 28

Sun 29

Notes
Lucky Numbers: 3, 93, 58, 91, 27, 81
Astrological Energy: Trusting
Color: Rose

March/April

Mon 30

Tues 31

Weds 1

First Quarter Moon in Cancer. 10.21 UTC
All Fools/April Fools Day

Thurs 2

April

Fri 3

Sat 4

Sun 5
Palm Sunday

Notes
Lucky Numbers: 3, 66, 5, 74, 53, 82
Astrological Energy: Celebratory
Color: Lemon

April

Mon 6

Tues 7

Weds 8
Full Moon in Libra, Supermoon. Pink Moon. 2:35 UTC
Passover (begins at sunset)

Thurs 9

April

Fri 10
Good Friday

Sat 11

Sun 12
Easter Sunday

Notes
Lucky Numbers: 86, 33, 34, 35, 75, 61
Astrological Energy: Harmonious
Color: Amber

April

Mon 13

Tues 14
Last Quarter Moon in Capricorn. 22.56 UTC

Weds 15

Thurs 16
Passover ends

April

Fri 17
Orthodox Good Friday

Sat 18

Sun 19
Orthodox Easter

Notes
Lucky Numbers: 37, 65, 90, 62, 99, 5
Astrological Energy: Inspiring
Color: Baby Blue

April

Mon 20

Tues 21

Weds 22
Lyrids Meteor Shower. April 16th-25th. Peaks night of April 22nd.
Earth Day

Thurs 23
New Moon in Taurus. 2:26 UTC
Ramadan Begins

April

Fri 24

Sat 25

Sun 26

Notes

Lucky Numbers: 88, 39, 83, 85, 26, 28
Astrological Energy: Committed
Color: Honeydew

April

Mon 27

Tues 28

Weds 29

Thurs 30
First Quarter Moon in Leo. 20.38 UTC

May

Fri 1
Beltane/May Day

Sat 2

Sun 3

Notes
Lucky Numbers: 18, 15, 51, 13, 41, 1
Astrological Energy: Complex
Color: Deep Pink

May

Mon 4

Tues 5

Weds 6
Eta Aquarids Meteor Shower. April 19th - May 28th. Peaks night of May 6th.

Thurs 7
Full Moon in Scorpio, Supermoon. Flower Moon. 10:45 UTC

May

Fri 8

Sat 9

Sun 10
Mother's Day

Notes
Lucky Numbers: 43, 65, 59, 5, 54, 34
Astrological Energy: Productive
Color: Forest Green

May

Mon 11

Tues 12

Weds 13

Thurs 14
Last Quarter Moon in Aquarius. 14.03 UTC

May

Fri 15

Sat 16

Sun 17

Notes

Lucky Numbers: 11, 68, 9, 39, 20, 88
Astrological Energy: Vibrant
Color: Aqua

May

Mon 18
Victoria Day (Canada)

Tues 19

Weds 20

Thurs 21

May

Fri 22
New Moon in Taurus. 17:39 UTC

Sat 23
Ramadan Ends

Sun 24

Notes
Lucky Numbers: 81, 34, 21, 97, 66, 43
Astrological Energy: Courageous
Color: Dark Violet

May

Mon 25
Memorial Day

Tues 26

Weds 27

Thurs 28
Shavuot (begins at sunset)

May

Fri 29

Sat 30
First Quarter Moon in Virgo. 3.30 UTC
Shavuot (ends at sunset)

Sun 31

Notes
Lucky Numbers: 29, 85, 92, 91, 60, 30
Astrological Energy: Complex
Color: Slate Blue

June

Mon 1

Tues 2

Weds 3

Thurs 4
Mercury at Greatest Eastern Elongation.

June

Fri 5
Full Moon in Sagittarius. Strawberry Moon. 19:12 UTC
Penumbral Lunar Eclipse.

Sat 6

Sun 7

Notes
Lucky Numbers: 74, 57, 56, 75, 67, 33
Astrological Energy: Daring
Color: Straw

June

Mon 8

Tues 9

Weds 10
Jupiter at Opposition.

Thurs 11

June

Fri 12

Sat 13
Last Quarter Moon in Pisces. 6.24 UTC

Sun 14
Flag Day

Notes
Lucky Numbers: 24, 61, 96, 42, 88, 47
Astrological Energy: Active
Color: Fire Brick

June

Mon 15

Tues 16

Weds 17
Mercury Retrograde begins.

Thurs 18

June

Fri 19

Sat 20

Sun 21

New Moon in Cancer. 6:41 UTC
Midsummer/Litha Solstice. 21:44 UTC
Annual Solar Eclipse.
Father's Day

Notes

Lucky Numbers: 21, 96, 92, 61, 36, 70
Astrological Energy: Exciting
Color: Cornflower Blue

June

Mon 22

Tues 23

Weds 24

Thurs 25

June

Fri 26

Sat 27

Sun 28
First Quarter Moon in Libra. 8.16 UTC

Notes
Lucky Numbers: 5, 91, 69, 39, 64, 6
Astrological Energy: Creative
Color: Red

June/July

Mon 29

Tues 30

Weds 1
Canada Day

Thurs 2

July

Fri 3
Independence Day (observed)

Sat 4
Independence Day

Sun 5
Full Moon in Capricorn. Buck Moon 4:44 UTC
Penumbral Lunar Eclipse.

Notes
Lucky Numbers: 58, 40, 99, 95, 18, 92
Astrological Energy: Curious
Color: Orange

July

Mon 6

Tues 7

Weds 8

Thurs 9

July

Fri 10

Sat 11

Sun 12

Last Quarter Moon in Aries. 23.29 UTC
Mercury Retrograde ends.

Notes

Lucky Numbers: 7, 36, 2, 20, 98 77
Astrological Energy: Stimulating
Color: Crimson

July

Mon 13

Tues 14
Jupiter at Opposition.

Weds 15

Thurs 16

July

Fri 17

Sat 18

Sun 19

Notes

Lucky Numbers: 82, 42, 66, 87, 42, 58
Astrological Energy: Inventive
Color: Ruby

July

Mon 20

New Moon in Cancer. 17:33 UTC
Saturn at Opposition.

Tues 21

Weds 22

Mercury at Greatest Western Elongation.

Thurs 23

July

Fri 24

Sat 25

Sun 26

Notes

Lucky Numbers: 31, 46, 25, 23, 43, 37
Astrological Energy: Methodical
Color: Peach

July/August

Mon 27

First Quarter Moon in Scorpio. 12.32 UTC

Tues 28

Delta Aquarids Meteor Shower. July 12th – Aug 23rd. Peaks night of July 28th.

Weds 29

Thurs 30

July/August

Fri 31

Sat 1
Lammas/Lughnasadh

Sun 2

Notes
Lucky Numbers: 35, 1, 7, 53, 26, 51
Astrological Energy: Constructive
Color: Lavender

August

Mon 3
Full Moon in Aquarius. Sturgeon Moon. 15:59 UTC

Tue 4

Wed 5

Thurs 6

August

Fri 7

Sat 8

Sun 9

Notes

Lucky Numbers: 30, 76, 90, 8, 41, 21
Astrological Energy: Independent
Color: Scarlet

August

Mon 10

Tues 11
Last Quarter Moon in Taurus. 16.45 UTC.

Weds 12
Perseids Meteor Shower. July 17th to August 24th. Peaks night of Aug 12th.

Thurs 13
Venus at Greatest Western Elongation.

August

Fri 14

Sat 15

Sun 16

Notes

Lucky Numbers: 65, 36, 98, 86, 47, 9
Astrological Energy: Aware
Color: Bronze

August

Mon 17

Tues 18

Weds 19
New Moon in Leo. 2:41 UTC

Thurs 20
Islamic New Year

August

Fri 21

Sat 22

Sun 23

Notes

Lucky Numbers: 40, 33, 63, 37, 45, 56
Astrological Energy: Spirited
Color: Mint

August

Mon 24

Tues 25

First Quarter Moon in Scorpio. 17.58 UTC

Weds 26

Thurs 27

August

Fri 28

Sat 29

Sun 30

Notes

Lucky Numbers: 22, 1, 30, 25, 2, 6
Astrological Energy: Enchanting
Color: Turquoise

August/September

Mon 31

Tues 1

Weds 2
Full Moon in Pisces. Full Corn Moon. 5:22 UTC

Thurs 3

September

Fri 4

Sat 5

Sun 6

Notes

Lucky Numbers: 86, 69, 78, 50, 71, 80
Astrological Energy: Unique
Color: Topaz

September

Mon 7
Labor Day

Tues 8

Weds 9

Thurs 10
Last Quarter Moon in Gemini. 9.26 UTC

September

Fri 11

Neptune at Opposition.

Sat 12

Sun 13

Notes

Lucky Numbers: 10, 12, 38, 62, 13, 91
Astrological Energy: Magnetic
Color: Coral

September

Mon 14

Tues 15

Weds 16

Thurs 17
New Moon in Virgo. 11:00 UTC

September

Fri 18

Rosh Hashanah (begins at sunset)

Sat 19

Sun 20

Rosh Hashanah (ends at sunset)

Notes

Lucky Numbers: 1, 54, 36, 80, 79, 57
Astrological Energy: Open
Color: White

September

Mon 21
International Day of Peace

Tues 22
Mabon/Fall Equinox. 13:31 UTC

Weds 23

Thurs 24
First Quarter Moon in Capricorn. 1.55 UTC

September

Fri 25

Sat 26

Sun 27
Yom Kippur (begins at sunset)

Notes
Lucky Numbers: 53, 89, 92, 97, 79, 71
Astrological Energy: Magical
Color: Maroon

September/October

Mon 28

Yom Kippur (ends at sunset)

Tues 29

Weds 30

Thurs 1

Full Moon in Aries. Harvest Moon. 21:05 UTC
Mercury at Greatest Eastern Elongation.

October

Fri 2
Sukkot (begins at sunset)

Sat 3

Sun 4

Notes
Lucky Numbers: 42, 11, 26, 5, 82, 14
Astrological Energy: Empathic
Color: Dark Orange

October

Mon 5

Tues 6

Weds 7

Draconids Meteor Shower. Oct 6th-10th. Peak night of Oct 7th.

Thurs 8

October

Fri 9
Sukkot (ends at sunset)

Sat 10
Last Quarter Moon in Cancer. 0.39 UTC

Sun 11

Notes
Lucky Numbers: 64, 1, 59, 48, 36, 61
Astrological Energy: Organized
Color: Chocolate

October

Mon 12

Columbus Day
Thanksgiving Day (Canada)
Indigenous People's Day

Tues 13

Mercury Retrograde begins.

Weds 14

Thurs 15

October

Fri 16

New Moon in Libra. 19:31 UTC

Sat 17

Sun 18

Notes

Lucky Numbers: 49, 37, 22, 78, 8, 4
Astrological Energy: Perceptive
Color: Salmon

October

Mon 19

Tues 20

Weds 21

Orionids Meteor Shower. Oct 2nd - Nov 7th. Peaks night of Nov 21st.

Thurs 22

October

Fri 23

First Quarter Moon in Capricorn. 13.23 UTC

Sat 24

Sun 25

Notes

Lucky Numbers: 96, 91, 20, 27, 33, 76
Astrological Energy: Mysterious
Color: Black

October

Mon 26

Tues 27

Weds 28

Thurs 29

October/November

Fri 30

Sat 31
Full Moon, Blue Moon in Taurus. Hunters Moon. 14:49 UTC
Uranus at Opposition.
Samhain/Halloween.

Sun 1
All Saints' Day

Notes
Lucky Numbers: 50, 44, 49, 97, 25, 1
Astrological Energy: Psychic
Color: Midnight

November

Mon 2

Tues 3
Mercury Retrograde ends.

Weds 4
Taurids Meteor Shower. Sept 7th - Dec 10th. Peaks on Nov 4th.

Thurs 5

November

Fri 6

Sat 7

Sun 8

Last Quarter Moon in Leo. 13.46 UTC

Notes

Lucky Numbers: 43, 18, 73, 51, 54, 92
Astrological Energy: Profound
Color: Royal Blue

November

Mon 9

Tues 10

Weds 11
Remembrance Day (Canada)
Veterans Day

Thurs 12

November

Fri 13

Sat 14

Sun 15
New Moon in Scorpio. 5:07 UTC

Notes
Lucky Numbers: 10, 7, 54, 57, 91, 21
Astrological Energy: Hectic
Color: Teal

November

Mon 16

Tues 17

Leonids Meteor Shower. Nov 6th-30th. Peaks night of Nov 17th.

Weds 18

Thurs 19

November

Fri 20

Sat 21

Sun 22
First Quarter Moon in Pisces. 4.45 UTC

Notes
Lucky Numbers: 75, 92, 5, 47, 99, 93
Astrological Energy: Structured
Color: Sky Blue

November

Mon 23

Tues 24

Weds 25

Thurs 26
Thanksgiving Day (US)

November

Fri 27

Sat 28

Sun 29

Notes

Lucky Numbers: 7, 25, 52, 75, 67, 55
Astrological Energy: Social
Color: Magenta

November/December

Mon 30

Full Moon in Gemini. Beaver Moon. 9:30 UTC
Penumbral Lunar Eclipse.

Tues 1

Weds 2

Thurs 3

December

Fri 4

Sat 5

Sun 6

Notes

Lucky Numbers: 87, 3, 92, 14, 83, 13
Astrological Energy: Impulsive
Color: Midnight Blue

December

Mon 7

Tues 8
Last Quarter Moon in Virgo. 0.37 UTC

Weds 9

Thurs 10
Hanukkah (begins at sunset)

December

Fri 11

Sat 12

Sun 13

Geminids Meteor Shower. Dec 7th-17th. Peaks nights of Dec 13th-15th.

Notes

Lucky Numbers: 67, 10, 7, 43, 76, 99
Astrological Energy: Vibrant
Color: Snow

December

Mon 14
New Moon in Sagittarius. 16:17 UTC

Tues 15

Weds 16

Thurs 17

December

Fri 18
Hanukkah (ends at sunset)

Sat 19

Sun 20

Notes
Lucky Numbers: 16, 85, 10, 96, 67, 1
Astrological Energy: Festive
Color: Powder Blue

December

Mon 21

Ursids Meteor Shower. Dec 17th – 25th. Peaks night of Dec 21st.
Great Conjunction of Jupiter and Saturn.
Yule/ Winter Solstice. 10:02 UTC
First Quarter Moon in Pisces. 23.41 UTC

Tues 22

Weds 23

Thurs 24

December

Fri 25
Christmas Day

Sat 26
Boxing Day (Canada & Uk)
Kwanzaa begins

Sun 27

Notes
Lucky Numbers: 33, 6, 30, 17, 80, 76
Astrological Energy: Graceful
Color: White

December

Mon 28

Tues 29

Weds 30
Full Moon in Cancer. Cold Moon. 3:28 UTC

Thurs 31
New Year's Eve

January

Fri 1
New Year's Day
Kwanzaa ends

Sat 2

Sun 3

Notes
Lucky Numbers: 23, 15, 12, 29, 71, 86
Astrological Energy: Aware
Color: Green Yellow

May the stars shine brightly in your world in 2020 and beyond.

About Crystal Sky

Crystal is passionate about the universe, helping others, and personal development. Crystal produces a range of astrologically minded diaries to celebrate the universal forces which affect us all. All reviews are read and appreciated.

Other Titles in the 2020 range:

Fairy Moon Diary 2020: Fairy Messages & Astrological Datebook
Shaman Moon Diary 2020: Shamanic Messages & Astrological Datebook

When not writing about the stars, you can find Crystal under them, gazing up at the abundance that surrounds us all, with her dog by her side.

www.ingramcontent.com/pod-product-compliance
Lightning Source LLC
Chambersburg PA
CBHW051802040426
42446CB00007B/476